A CHILD'S GUIDE

to the

𝒲estminster

Shorter Catechism

James R. Boyd

Bibliographic Information

This edition was previously published in 1855 under the full title, *The Child's Book on the Westminster Shorter Catechism: Forming an Easy Introduction and Help for Understanding That Work, and Committing it to Memory* by the Presbyterian Board of Publication in Philadelphia. Spelling, language, and grammar has been gently updated.

Copyright © 2015 Ichthus Publications
ISBN 13: 978-1514171103
ISBN 10: 1514171104

www.ichthuspublications.com

Contents

Note to the Reader

AS TO THE *best manner of using this little volume*, it is recommend that the child be not required to commit to memory any of the answers preliminary to those of the Assembly's Catechism; but merely to read them aloud to the parent, or teacher, very deliberately, several times; as, by adopting this course, the main answer will be intelligently, and thus easily and pleasantly, committed to memory in a short period.

The author thinks that parents might profitably use, with their children, this little volume half an hour of each Sabbath, *as a reading book*, for the purpose also of a *brief review of the system of Divine truth*, it will readily suggest useful religious conversation, and thus promote the spiritual interests of the family. It may be used, in like manner, *in the Sabbath-school*—so that, in a few Sabbaths, the whole outline of Divine truth, and the technical terms of theological teachings, may be made familiar to the youthful mind.

A Child's Guide

to the

Westminster Shorter Catechism

THE PURPOSE FOR WHICH MAN WAS MADE

Q. Who made you?
A. God.

Q. What did he make you for?
A. He made me for more than one *end*, or purpose; but his highest purpose in making me was to glorify God and enjoy him forever.

Q. What does it mean to *glorify* God?
A. It is to honor, love, and serve him.

Q. What does it mean to *enjoy* God?
A. It is to have his friendship and love, and thus to be as happy as possible.

Q. For how long a time are you to honor God, and thus be happy in his favor?
A. *Forever*.

Q. What does all this teach you?

A. (1) That I am to thank God that he has made me for so high and good a purpose, and that I must make it my sincere business to do what he made me for.

(2) I must be thankful that God has made me to live forever, and to live in the happiest manner possible, if I love and obey him in this short life on earth.

THEREFORE,

Q.1. What is Man's Chief End?

Man's chief end is to glorify God and to enjoy Him forever.

THE RULE BY WHICH MAN IS TO GLORIFY GOD

Q. Does man, of himself, know how to glorify God and enjoy him?

A. He does not; he needs some *rule*, some *directions*.

Q. Has God given any such rule? Has he spoken or written to us on the subject?

A. He has spoken or written to us all that we need to know. The Bible is called the *Word of God*, because he has therein spoken to us. It is called the *Scriptures*, or writings, because he has therein written to us. They were written with the pen at first, and continued to be thus written until the art of printing was invented in the fifteenth century.

Q. Did God write them himself, or cause men to write them?

A. Except the Ten Commandments, which he himself wrote, all the Bible was written by good men, whom he directed and taught what to write; so that what they have written has the same authority and value as if God had himself written it.

Q. Into what parts is the Word of God divided?

A. Into the *Old* and *New Testaments*.

Q. What books does the Old Testament contain?

A. Thirty-nine books beginning with Genesis and ending with Malachi (see the Bible).

Q. What books does the New Testament contain?

A. Twenty-seven books beginning with Matthew and ending with Revelation (see the Bible).

Q. What does the word *Testament* here mean?

A. It means the same as the word *covenant*, agreement, method of proceeding, plan of action, system of instruction and religious service.

Q. What is the Old Testament sometimes called?
A. It is called the *Mosaic Dispensation*, as it contains the writings, the laws, and the religious ceremonies given by Moses.

Q. What is the New Testament sometimes called?
A. The New, or Gospel Dispensation; sometimes the *Christian Dispensation*; being that system of doctrine, and worship, and salvation which was brought in by Jesus Christ.

Q. Who were the writers of the Old and New Covenants?
A. Moses and the Prophets wrote the books contained in the former; the Evangelists and Apostles wrote those of the latter.

Q. How then are you to read their writings?
A. I am to read them with great attention and seriousness, and with a readiness to believe what they teach, and to obey what they command, as proceeding from the high and awful authority of God; as being *his word* to me.

Q. Is there *no other* rule of conduct but the Bible?

A. This is the only infallible, Divine rule which I am bound to obey; and whatever disagrees with it is to be disregarded or rejected.

THEREFORE,

Q. 2. What Rule has God Given to direct us how we may glorify and enjoy him?

The Word of God, which is contained in the Scriptures of the Old and New Testaments, is the only rule to direct us how we may glorify and enjoy him.

THE PRINCIPAL INSTRUCTIONS OF THE
HOLY SCRIPTURES

Q. Are all the teachings of the Bible of equal importance?
A. Some are of greater value and worthy of more particular attention than others.

Q. What are the *principal* or more valuable parts of the Word of God?
A. Those which teach me *what things I am to believe concerning God, and what God commands me to be and to do*; in other words, what my *duty* is.

Q. Are these parts to receive my greatest attention?

A. As they deserve it, so should they receive it; and such is God's desire, and my own advantage.

THEREFORE,

Q. 3. What do the Scriptures principally teach?

The Scriptures principally teach what man is to believe concerning God, and what duty God requires of man.

NATURE AND PERFECTIONS OF GOD

Q. What is a *spirit*?

A. It is a *being* that has none of the properties of matter; is without a body.

Q. What is *infinite*?

A. It is that which has no limits or bounds; is vast and inconceivably great.

Q. What is *eternal*?

A. It is that which has always existed, and always shall exist.

Q. What is *unchangeable*?

A. That which has always been and always shall be what it now is; having the same nature and properties.

Q. What kind of a being is God?

A. God is *a spirit, infinite, eternal, and unchangeable*; he is without a body; he is confined to no particular space, nor has he any limits; he always existed, and always will exist; and in no respect different from what he now is and ever has been.

Q. In what particulars is God infinite, eternal, and unchangeable?

A. He is so in his *being*, or manner of existence, or nature, as superior to all other beings.

Q. In what other particulars is God infinite, eternal, and unchangeable?

A. In his wisdom, power, holiness, justice, goodness, and truth.

Q. What is the *wisdom* of God?

A. It means not only knowledge, but *the right and best use of his boundless stores of knowledge*. He knows all things, and he turns his knowledge to the best account.

Q. What is the *power* of God?

A. It is the ability which he has to do what he desires or purposes to do.

Q. What is the *holiness* of God?

A. The holiness of God is his entire freedom from everything wrong in feeling and in action. He is incapable of loving or doing anything that is unworthy of himself, and of the honor of his great name. His holiness causes him, likewise, to hate and to oppose all that is wrong in the feelings or conduct of his creatures; and, on the other hand, to be pleased with all that is right and pure.

Q. What is the *justice* of God?

A. The justice of God causes him to do what is right to his creatures, and to demand of them what is due to himself, and to punish them when they refuse to render it.

Q. What is the *goodness* of God?

A. The goodness of God is that perfection by which he is prompted to use means for making his creatures happy.

Q. What do you understand by the *truth* of God?

A. The *truth* or *faithfulness* of God is that perfection by which he cares to do all that he has promised or threatened; so that what he has said may ever be relied upon; and "thus saith the Lord" is the surest thing in the universe.

Q. What do you learn from the above statements?

A. I learn that God is the most interesting being in the universe; the most to be studied, honored, loved, and feared.

THEREFORE,

Q. 4. What is God?

God is a spirit, infinite, eternal, and unchangeable, in his being, wisdom, power, holiness, justice, goodness and truth.

UNITY OF GOD

Q. How many Gods are there, such as is described in the last answer?
A. There is only one God.

Q. Are there not other *beings* or *things* that are called "gods," and worshiped as such?
A. Yes, a vast number, and of great variety.

Q. What names are applied to such in the Bible?
A. They are called *idols*, *vanity*, a *lie*.

Q. How do they differ from God as described above?
A. They either do not exist, but are merely imagined to

exist; or they are only created things, animate or inanimate, and there is no reason why they should be honored and worshiped as gods.

Q. How is God described, in opposition to them?
A. He is described as the *only* God, as the *living* God, as the *true God.*

Q. Why is he called the *only* God?
A. Because there are no other beings worthy of the name or place of God.

Q. Why is he called the *living* God?
A. Not only in contrast with the gods which the heathen worship, and which are without life, and without understanding, but because he is the great author and preserver of the life of every living creature, and he gave existence to all things.

Q. Why is he called the *true* God?
A. Because all other beings that are called and regarded as gods, *are not really such*; they are *false* gods; those who worship them are *deceived.*

Q. Is it a common thing to worship these dead and false gods?
A. It is indeed that several billion people pay all their religious respect and worship to no other god than such miserable things as these.

Q. What do such deluded people need?

A. They need the Holy Scriptures to direct them to give up such a degrading sort of worship, and to lift up their hearts to that great, and good, and supreme Being, whom we are taught to look up to as our God and alone worthy to be the God of all men.

HOW, THEN, DO YOU REPLY TO THE QUESTION,

Q. 5. Are there more Gods than one?

There is but one only, the living and true God.

THE DOCTRINE OF THE TRINITY

Q. While there is but one God, what interesting fact do the Scriptures reveal about his manner of existing, or his nature?

A. They speak of the Godhead as including the *Father*, the *Son*, and the *Holy Spirit*.

Q. Is the *Father* God?

A. Yes, but not separate from the Son and the Holy Spirit.

Q. Is the *Son* God?

19

A. Yes, but not exclusive of the Father and the Holy Spirit.

Q. Is the *Holy Spirit* God?
A. Yes, but not to the exclusion of the Father and of the Son.

Q. Do these make three gods?
A. No; they together make one divine, supreme Being, yet the Father is God, the Son is God, the Holy Spirit is God?

Q. What are these called?
A. They are called the *persons* of the Godhead.

Q. Is the word "person" used in the same sense as when we apply it to one another?
A. Not at all; but merely to show that there is a threefold difference in the manner of God's existence.

Q. Is this a fact which we are able to comprehend?
A. No; it is above the comprehension of the wisest man.

Q. Why then are you required to believe the fact?
A. Because God, who alone understands his own great nature, so describes himself in the Bible, as God the Father, Son, and Holy Spirit.

Q. Is the substance of the Father, Son and Spirit, the same?

A. Yes, it is the same substance.

Q. Is there any difference between the Father, Son and Spirit, as to power, excellence, worthiness, and greatness? **A.** Not at all, for the names, the qualities, the works, the worship peculiar to God are ascribed equally to the Father, to the Son, and to the Holy Spirit.

T H E R E F O R E,

Q. 6. How many persons are there in the Godhead?

There are three persons in the Godhead: the Father, the Son, and the Holy Spirit; and these three (persons) are one God, the same in substance, equal in power and glory.

THE DECREES OF GOD

Q. Has God anything to do with what comes to pass? **A.** Yes; he knows beforehand *all* that will come to pass.

Q. Does he do anything to cause it to come to pass?

A. Yes; he either causes it by his own power and wisdom, or he chooses that it shall take place by means of other beings.

Q. Has he any plan laid down in his own infinite mind, any settled thoughts as to what shall actually take place and as to what shall not take place?

A. He has such a plan, such a *purpose*.

Q. When did he form it? When did he arrange in his own mind what should take place?

A. He always had such a plan; his purpose concerning things future *always existed* in his mind; that is, it was an *eternal purpose*. What he now determines or purposes, he always determined or purposed to do, or to allow to be done.

Q. Were his purposes or intentions formed by the advice of any other being?

A. Not at all; they were formed before any other being lived, and by himself and as he himself chose; that is, *according to the counsel of his own will*; not as other beings might will for him.

Q. What guided him in forming his plans or purposes?

A. He sought to gain honor or *glory* to himself, in what he purposed or *foreordained* to come to pass.

Q. Is this the highest and best reason for what God has done in bringing about or allowing events to happen as they do?

A. There can be no object more important than that God, the greatest and best of beings, should make himself known, and duly honored, and obeyed, and loved among his intelligent creatures.

THEREFORE,

Q. 7. What are the decrees of God?

The decrees of God are his eternal purpose, according to the counsel of his will, whereby, for his own glory, he hath foreordained whatsoever comes to pass.

EXECUTION OF GOD'S DECREES

Q. What works of God are there?

A. Those of Creation and of Providence.

Q. Do his *decrees* or purposes relate to these works?

A. In these works he *executes* or brings to pass what he has purposed or foreordained.

Q. 8. How does God execute his decrees?

God executes his decrees in the works of creation and providence.

THE CREATION OF THE WORLD

Q. Who made all things?
A. God.

Q. Of what did he make them?
A. Out of *nothing*; there was at first nothing to make them out of.

Q. How did he make them?
A. By the *power of his word*; by his simple command. He merely put forth his power, and they came into being as he willed that they should.

Q. For how long a time was he employed in creating the world?
A. The space of *six days*.

Q. What was the nature of all things when they came from the hands of the Creator?

A. They were *all very good*; they answered the purpose for which God made them; they were just as they should be. The world was well made and did honor to the Maker.

T H E R E F O R E,

Q. 9. What is the work of creation?

The work of creation is God's making all things of nothing, by the word of his power, in the space of six days—and all very good.

THE CREATION OF MAN

Q. After whose *image*, or likeness, did God make the first man and woman?

A. After his own image; in their character and station they greatly resembled their Creator.

Q. In what respects did they resemble God?

A. In *knowledge*, *righteousness*, and *holiness*; that is, they were knowing, righteous, and holy beings, and, so far, were altogether superior to other creatures on earth.

Q. In what other respect did they resemble God?

A. In the *dominion*, or rule, which God gave them over the other creatures and things on earth. They had authority to make use of them according to their wants, and creatures were made obedient to their wishes in this respect.

THEREFORE,

Q. 10. How did God create mankind?

God created mankind, male and female, after his own image, in knowledge, righteousness, and holiness, with dominion over the creatures.

GOD'S GENERAL PROVIDENCE

Q. Does God *preserve* and *govern* all his creatures?

A. He keeps them in existence, and supplies their wants; he has them at all times in his power, and by means of them carries out his plans, and does what he chooses to do with them.

Q. Does God govern the *actions* of his creatures?

A. All their actions are under his direction and rule so that they can do nothing except as he pleases to let them, and even their bad actions he is able to turn to a good result.

Q. What can be said of the *manner* in which God preserves and governs his creatures and their actions?
A. It is *most holy, wise, and powerful.* Such is the *providence of God.*

THEREFORE,

Q. 11. What are God's works of providence?

God's works of providence are his most holy, wise, and powerful preserving and governing all his creatures and all their actions.

THE COVENANT OF WORKS

Q. After man was created, what covenant or agreement did God make with him?
A. He entered into a *covenant of life* with him.

Q. Why was this agreement called a covenant *of life*?

A. Because *life* was promised and secured to man, if he should do what it required.

Q. What was the *condition*, that is, what was to be done by man that life might be secured to him?

A. The condition was *perfect obedience*; man was to act fully and constantly according to the requirement of the covenant.

Q. What was the requirement?

A. That man should not eat of the fruit of a certain tree in the garden called the tree of the knowledge of good and evil.

Q. Why was it so called?

A. Because the eating of that fruit, after God had forbidden it, brought man to know, by feeling, the different effects of doing good and of doing evil.

Q. What bad effect was to follow upon disobeying God in this particular?

A. Man became subject to death.

Q. What *good* effect would follow if man had refused to eat of that tree?

A. His life, and innocence, and happiness, would always have continued.

THEREFORE,

Q. 12. What particular and important act of providence did God exercise toward man in the state wherein he was created?

When God had created man he entered into a covenant of life with him, upon condition of perfect obedience; forbidding him to eat of the tree of the knowledge of good and evil, upon the pain of death.

MAN'S DISOBEDIENCE AND FALL BY SIN

Q. Did our first parents obey God in regard to the fruit of the tree?

A. No: they *sinned against God.*

Q. How did this happen?

A. They were *left to the freedom of their own will*; that is, were left to do as they pleased, were not compelled to do right, or as God directed.

Q. What happened when they transgressed the rule of action which God gave them?

A. They *fell from the estate in which they were created*; that is, they were no longer in a state of innocence and happiness.

Q. 13. Did our first parents continue in the state wherein they were created?

Our first parents, being left to the freedom of their own will, fell from the estate wherein they were created, by sinning against God.

NATURE OF SIN IN GENERAL

Q. When we neglect or fail to do what God requires, what may we call such conduct?
A. It is *a want of conformity to the law* of God, a want of obedience to it.

Q. When we do that which God forbids, what may the act be called?
A. It is a *transgression of the law*, a *going beyond* what it allows.

Q. What is either of these kinds of conduct called?
A. It is called *sin*.

THEREFORE,

Q. 14. What is sin?

Sin is any want of conformity unto, or transgression of the law of God.

NATURE OF ADAM'S SIN, IN PARTICULAR

Q. What was the first sin?
A. Eating of the *forbidden* fruit.

Q. What was implied in this sin?
A. Our first parents thereby lost their innocence, so that their state or mode of life became sadly different from what it was at first.

THEREFORE,

Q. 15. What was the sin whereby our first parents fell from the estate wherein they were created?

The sin whereby our first parents fell from the estate wherein they were created was their eating the forbidden fruit.

Q. Did Adam's sin and fall stop with himself?

A. His sin and fall included the sin and fall of his children, and of all that should descend from him in the ordinary way.

Q. Have any persons descended from him in any other way?

A. Jesus Christ was born in a peculiar and extraordinary manner.

Q. Why was this?

A. Because it was necessary for him, as a Savior, that he should be born without a sinful nature.

Q. How did it happen that because Adam sinned and fell from innocence, all mankind should become sinners also and exposed to misery?

A. Because the covenant, or agreement, about the tree of knowledge of good and evil, related not only to Adam, but to all mankind that should come after him in the common way.

Q. What do you mean by this?

A. I mean, that if Adam had continued obedient to God, as long as God chose to try him, it would happen that they would be born with a sinless nature and remain in an innocent and happy condition. But on the other hand, if Adam should prove disobedient, they would possess his nature in its changed and fallen state. Thus it appears that he acted not for himself alone, but for them also. It was appointed that his conduct would affect their character and condition.

THEREFORE,

Q. 16. Did all mankind fall in Adam's first transgression?

The covenant being made with Adam, not only for himself, but for his posterity, all mankind descending from him by ordinary generation sinned in him, and fell with him in his first transgression.

CONSEQUENCES OF THE FALL

Q. What does sin lead to?

A. Sin leads to *misery*; it leads to *pain* and *death*.

Q. What is meant by the *fall* of Adam?

A. It means his descending, by his first sin, from a higher to a lower condition; from a better to a worse; from a right to a wrong state.

Q. 17. Into what state did the fall bring mankind?

The fall brought mankind into a state of sin and misery.

THE SINFULNESS OF MAN'S STATE BY THE FALL

Q. What state did Adam's first sin bring man into?
A. Into a *state of sinfulness*.

Q. What does that sinfulness consist in?
A. First, in the *guilt of Adam s first sin*.

Q. What do you mean by this?
A. I mean that, on account of that sin, we are made liable to sorrow and death as if we had ourselves committed it.

Q. What else is included in the sinfulness of mankind?
A. The *want of original righteousness*.

Q. What do you mean by this?
A. The want of that entire goodness or rightness of character which Adam had when he was created.

Q. Does the sinfulness of man include anything else?

A. It includes *the corruption of his whole nature*.

Q. What do you mean by this?
A. By this I mean that man, as to the body and soul, is in an unsound and diseased condition. He does not act as Adam at first did. At first he was perfect; his decisions and actions were all right; but since his fall the powers of mind and body tend to a bad use; tend to unlawful action.

Q. What is this *corruption* commonly called.
A. It is commonly called *original sin*, or the sin that is *born with us*; it may be regarded as a part of our nature or constitution. It is not learned by imitation of others, though it may be thereby increased. It is natural to us. It comes to us without any effort on our part.

Q. Does the sinfulness of our estate embrace anything besides the three particulars mentioned already?
A. It embraces also the *actual transgressions* which proceed from the corruption or depravity of our whole nature. It embraces *all the sinful acts* which we commit.

THEREFORE,

Q. 18. Wherein consists the sinfulness of the estate whereinto man fell?

The sinfulness of that estate whereinto man fell consists in the guilt of Adam's first sin, the want of original righteousness, and the corruption of his whole nature, which is commonly called "original sin," together with all actual transgressions which proceed from it.

THE MISERY OF MAN S STATE BY THE FALL

Q. What did all mankind lose by the fall of Adam?
A. They *lost communion with God*; they lost his friendship, his gracious presence, and favor.

Q. What did the fall bring mankind under?
A. The fall brought mankind *under the wrath and curse of God*; under God's displeasure, and under the condemning sentence of his law.

Q. To what were mankind thus exposed or *made liable*?
A. They were made liable *to all* the miseries, or evils, of this life, to death itself, and to the pains of hell forever.

THEREFORE,

Q. 19. What is the misery of that state whereinto man fell?

All mankind by their fall lost communion with God, are under his wrath and curse, and so made liable to all the miseries of this life, to death itself, and to the pains of hell forever.

THE PLAN OF REDEMPTION

Q. To what did God *elect*, or choose *some* men?
A. God elected *some* men *to everlasting life*.

Q. When did he do this?
A. *From all eternity*; that is, God has always chosen some men to everlasting life.

Q. On what account? Was it for the sake of anything good in them, or of anything done?
A. It was *out of his mere good pleasure*; it was only because he saw it proper, or best to do so; it was for reasons which he has not made known; it must have been for good reasons.

Q. What did this election of some men to everlasting life lead God to do?
A. It led him to enter into a *Covenant of Grace*.

Q. What is meant by this expression?

A. An agreement, or plan, showing the greatest kindness and undeserved favor to the ill-deserving.

Q. What was the object of this covenant or gracious plan?
A. The object of the Covenant of Grace was *to deliver* those who were elected to everlasting life *out of the estate of sin and misery*, and to *bring them into* the opposite *state of salvation*.

Q. By means of whom were the elect to be thus delivered and saved?
A. By *a Redeemer*.

THEREFORE,

Q. 20. Did God leave all mankind to perish in the estate of sin and misery?

God, having out of his mere good pleasure, from all eternity, elected some to everlasting life, did enter into a Covenant of Grace to deliver them out of the estate of sin and misery, and to bring them into a state of salvation, by a Redeemer.

THE PERSON AND CHARACTER OF THE REDEEMER

Q. Who is *the Redeemer* of God's elect?

A. The *Lord Jesus Christ* is the Redeemer, and the *only Redeemer* of God's elect.

Q. Who is the Lord Jesus Christ?
A. The Lord Jesus Christ is the *eternal Son of God.*

Q. Did he become anything else than God?
A. He, while he was the eternal Son of God, *became* man.

Q. Was the Lord Jesus Christ *both* God and man?
A. He *was,* and he *continues to be* God and man.

Q. Is his nature as God mixed with his nature as man?
A. The *divine* and *human* natures of Christ are distinct.

Q. Does Christ exist in two persons?
A. Christ exists in *one person* or being.

Q. How long will he have the two natures of God and man, and how long will he exist in one person?
A. *Forever*.

THEREFORE,

Q. 21. Who is the Redeemer of God's elect?

The only Redeemer of God's elect is the Lord Jesus Christ, who, being the eternal Son of God, became man, and so was and continues to be God and man in two distinct natures and one person, forever.

Q. How did *Christ*, who was the *Son of God, become man*?
A. Christ *took to himself*, or joined to himself, *a true* or real *body*, and a *reasonable* (or rational) *soul*, thus making up a complete man—all that belongs to a man.

Q. How was Christ, as a man, born?
A. The human soul and body of Christ were formed in an extraordinary and miraculous manner, *by the power of the Holy Spirit in the womb of the Virgin Mary, and born of her.*

Q. Was he born with such a moral nature as persons who are born in the usual way?
A. His human nature was produced and begotten in this peculiar way that it might be *without sin.*

THEREFORE,

Q. 22. How did Christ, being the Son of God, become man?

Christ, the Son of God, became man by taking to himself a true body and a reasonable soul; being conceived by the power of the Holy Spirit in the womb of the Virgin Mary, and born of her, yet without sin.

THE OFFICES OF THE REDEEMER

Q. As our Redeemer what *offices*, or duties, does Christ *execute*, or fulfill?

A. Those of a *prophet*, of a *priest*, and of *king*.

Q. In what states or conditions does he execute those offices; in other words, where does he act as a prophet, priest, and king?

A. In his *estate of humiliation and of exaltation*; that is, during his residence on earth and since he returned to heaven.

THEREFORE,

Q. 23. What offices does Christ execute as our Redeemer?

Christ, as our Redeemer, executes the offices of a prophet, of a priest, and of a king, both in his estate of humiliation and of exaltation.

Q. What does Christ, as a *prophet*, reveal to us?

A. He *reveals*, or makes known to us, *the will of God*; what God would have us to know and to do.

Q. How does he reveal to us the will of God?

A. By his *Word and Spirit*, by the *sacred Scriptures*, and by the unseen influences of the *Holy Spirit* upon our minds and hearts, by which we are made to understand and to feel the force of what the Scriptures contain.

Q. *Why* does Christ thus make known to us the will of God?

A. He makes it known to us *for our salvation*; we could not otherwise be saved; and hence we ought most highly to regard and attend to what we are taught by the Word and Spirit of the living God.

Q. What salvation is intended?

A. A deliverance from sin, and from misery, to a certain extent in this life, but fully and forever in the next.

THEREFORE,

Q. 24. How does Christ execute (or perform) the office of a prophet?

Christ executes the office of a prophet in revealing to us, by his Word and Spirit, the will of God for our salvation.

CHRIST'S PRIESTLY OFFICE

Q. As a priest, *what* did Christ do?
A. He *offered up himself* as *a sacrifice* on the cross; he gave his life for us.

Q. For what purpose did he do this?
A. To *satisfy* divine justice, and to *reconcile* us to God.

Q. What is meant by his satisfying divine justice?
A. He obeyed and suffered all that the law and justice of God required of him, as standing in the place of those for whom he died.

Q. What is meant by his *reconciling us to God*?
A. From enemies to God we become friends, and are treated as such; we enjoy the favor of God.

Q. What other thing does Christ do, as our priest?
A. He *makes continual intercession* for us. He prays for us; he, in heaven, is always helping on our salvation.

Q. Is there any other priest but Christ able to perform these duties?

A. There is none other. He alone can do what has now been ascribed to him.

THEREFORE,

Q. 25. How does Christ execute the office of a priest?

Christ executes the office of a priest in his once offering up of himself a sacrifice to satisfy divine justice, and reconcile us to God, and in making continual intercession for us.

CHRIST'S KINGLY OFFICE

Q. What does Christ execute or do for us as a king?

A. (1) He *subdues us to himself*, if we belong to his people; he makes us willingly to obey his commands.

(2) He *rules us*; he gives us laws; he declares what we may do, and what we may not do.

(3) He *defends us* from those beings and things that might injure or destroy us; from Satan, from wicked men, and from sin.

(4) He *restrains his own enemies*, which are also *our enemies*; he does not permit them to carry out fully their wicked plans; he hinders or overcomes them.

(5) He *conquers those enemies*, both his and ours.

THEREFORE,

Q. 26. How does Christ execute the office of a king?

Christ executes the office of a king, in subduing us to himself, in ruling and defending us, and in restraining and conquering all his and our enemies.

OF CHRIST'S STATE OF HUMILIATION

Q. What do you mean by the *humiliation* of Christ?
A. I understand by it, his putting himself in a lower condition than that which he had always had in heaven.

Q. In what did this lower condition consist?
A. It consisted *in his being born*; in his becoming the babe of Bethlehem. It also consisted in his being *born in a low condition*; in a state of poverty, a poor virgin being his mother, a stable his birthplace, and a manger his cradle.

45

Q. What was the next thing showing that Christ humbled himself?

A. He was *made under the law*; he set himself to obey the law in our place, as a Covenant of Works, to obey all its commands, and to suffer pains to which the transgressor was exposed.

Q. How did this conduct humble Christ?

A. It will be seen, when we remember that Christ was himself the *lawgiver* and *judge* of man; was, as God, above the law, was under no obligation to obey it, but became subject to his own law, that he might deliver his people from the punishment which threatened them for transgressing it, and that he might so fulfill its commands in their place, that they might, for his sake, be treated as righteous.

Q. How does it further appear that Christ humbled himself when he became subject to the law?

A. It appears from his thus *undergoing*, or suffering, the *miseries of this life*, such as hunger, thirst, weariness, grief, and so on.

Still more, it appears in giving himself up to the *wrath of God*, the displeasure of God, because he stood in our place as sinners, and was made to feel, as directed against himself, that divine displeasure which was due to us.

Q. Did Christ humble himself in any other respects?

A. He submitted to the degrading and painful, the *cursed death of the cross*, which was a terrible instrument of torture, and usually employed only for the greatest criminals.

Q. What was the last step of *humiliation*? It consisted in his *being buried, and continuing under the power of death for a time*; in his consenting to remain dead, and to be held as prisoner in the grave until the third day after his crucifixion.

THEREFORE,

Q. 27. Wherein did Christ's humiliation consist?

Christ's humiliation consisted in his being born, and that in a low condition; made under the law, undergoing the miseries of this life, the wrath of God, and the cursed death of the cross; in being buried, and continuing under the power of death for a time.

Q. Having looked at Christ when he reached his lowest place, that is, in the grave, what is the first step in his *exaltation*?

A. The *first* step was *his rising again from the dead on the third day* to the condition of a living person.

Q. What was the *second* step?

A. It was *his ascending up into heaven* with his human nature.

Q. What was the *third* step?

A. It was *his sitting at the right hand* of God the Father.

Q. What does this expression mean?

A. As God the Father has no body, or bodily parts, it simply means that Christ was raised to the highest honor, power, and authority in heaven.

Q. Is there not *another* step of exaltation yet to be taken by the Redeemer?

A. He will come to *judge the world* at the last day; to decide upon the character and everlasting state of each person in the human family; to sentence each one to everlasting life or everlasting death.

THEREFORE,

Q. 28. Wherein did Christ's exaltation consist?

Christ's exaltation consisted in his rising again from the dead on the third day, in ascending up into heaven, in sitting at the right hand of God the Father, and in coming to judge the world at the last day.

THE AGENT BY WHOM REDEMPTION IS APPLIED

Q. What has Christ *purchased* for us?

A. Christ has purchased *redemption*, which means deliverance, by paying a price.

Q. Deliverance from what?

A. From all evil, from sin and punishment; and besides this, redemption includes the bestowing of all good, especially the blessings of the life eternal.

Q. How do we come to *partake of*, or possess, this redemption?

A. We are *mode partakers* of it by the *Holy Spirit*. He *makes application of it*, or applies it to us. He *effectually*, that is, really, brings us into such a state of mind and heart that we are *benefited*, or saved, by what Christ has done for us.

Q. Why is the Spirit of God called the *Holy* Spirit.

A. Because he is pure and good in his own nature, and because the object of his exertions in the hearts of men is to make them pure and good also.

Q. Why is he called *His* (Christ's) Holy Spirit?

A. Because, although he is also the Spirit of the Father, yet in applying redemption he is more directly sent by Christ.

THEREFORE,

Q. 29. How are we made partakers of the redemption purchased by Christ?

We are made partakers of the redemption purchased by Christ, by the effectual application of it to us by his Holy Spirit.

THE METHOD OF APPLYING REDEMPTION

Q. *How* does the Spirit apply *redemption* to us?

A. He applies redemption by *working faith in us*; by causing us to believe and trust in what Christ, as our redeemer, has done.

Q. What is the *effect of the faith* which the Spirit produces in us?

A. It *unites us to Christ*; it so connects us with him that as doings and sufferings, in our place, are regarded as our doings and sufferings.

Q. When does this union to Christ take place?

A. It takes place in our *effectual calling*.

THEREFORE,

Q. 30. How does the Spirit apply to us the redemption purchased by Christ?

The Spirit applies to us the redemption purchased by Christ, by working faith in us, and thereby uniting us to Christ in our effectual calling.

THE APPLICATION OF REDEMPTION IN
EFFECTUAL CALLING

Q. Whose work is effectual calling?

A. It is the *work of God s Spirit*; he performs it.

Q. What other calling is there?
A. That which is merely outward; invitations read or heard only from the Word of God, but not accepted or acted upon by the sinner.

Q. In effectual calling what does the Spirit do?
A. He *first convinces us of sin*; makes us feel that we are sinners, that we have transgressed God's law, and wherein we have transgressed it.

Q. What else does he convince us of?
A. He *convinces us of our misery*; of our having brought ourselves into a wretched state by our sins; of our being exposed to the punishment of everlasting death, and of our deserving it.

Q. What light does the Spirit convey to our minds?
A. He *enlightens our minds* in the knowledge of Christ; he holds Christ up to our view in his true character, in his offices of prophet, priest, and king, in his invitations and commands, in his ability and willingness to save.

Q. Does the Spirit have anything to do with our *wills*?
A. He *renews our wills*; he causes us to will, or choose rightly in view of sin and the misery resulting from it, and of Christ as our redeemer from both.

Q. What is the *result* of the aforesaid acts of the Spirit?

A. He *persuades and enables us to embrace* Jesus Christ; to give him and his promises such regard, and confidence, and honor, as our salvation requires.

Q. Under what form or circumstance is Christ thus *embraced*?

A. He is embraced, or accepted, as *freely offered in the Gospel*; as offered without any compensation or pay on our part; offered without money and without price.

He has himself paid for the unspeakably valuable blessings which he offers to us, but they are offered to us *without price*. He requires of us no works, no sacrifices, in order to *entitle* us to be saved by him, or to recommend us to him. We are, and always must be, entirely *unworthy* of Christ's favor and of the redemption he has purchased for us.

Q. What is meant by the *Gospel*?

A. It means the *good news* or *good history* which the New Testament bears to us concerning Christ, as an almighty and willing Savior. It embraces all the New Testament, and some parts of the Old.

THEREFORE,

Q. 31. What is effectual calling?

Effectual calling is the work of God's Spirit, whereby, convincing us of our sin and misery, enlightening our minds in the knowledge of Christ, and renewing our wills, he persuades and enables us to embrace Jesus Christ, freely offered to us in the Gospel.

BENEFITS OF REDEMPTION IN THIS LIFE

Q. Of what advantage is it to be *called* in the way just described?

A. It is of great advantage to us even *in this life*; for thus we obtain *justification*, *adoption*, and *sanctification*.

Q. Do we obtain anything else?

A. We obtain *several benefits*, or blessings, which in this life do either accompany or flow from them.

THEREFORE,

Q. 32. What benefits do they that are effectually called partake of in this life?

They that are effectually called do in this life partake of justification, adoption, and sanctification, and the several benefits which in this life do either accompany or flow from them.

OF JUSTIFICATION

Q. What is meant by the words *free grace*?

A. They mean *undeserved favor* or *kindness*.

Q. What is meant by the expression *God pardons all our sins*?

A. It means, God has decided not to punish us for our sins.

Q. What is meant when it is said that *he accepts us as righteous in his sight*?

A. It means that he treats us as kindly and lovingly *as if* we had always obeyed his laws.

Q. On what account does God thus pardon all our sins and accept us as if we were righteous persons?

A. He does it only on account of the righteousness of Christ.

Q. In what did the righteousness of Christ consist?

A. It consisted in his obeying the commands of the law in our place and in suffering the penalty, or what is equal to it.

Q. How do we come to be benefited by the righteousness of Christ?

A. It is *imputed to us*; it is reckoned as *our* righteousness, though it is not in fact ours. That is, we are treated as if we had been in the place of Christ in obeying the law and suffering the penalty; or as if we had never disobeyed the law or deserved the punishment it threatens.

Q. But what must we do that the righteousness of Christ may be thus imputed or reckoned to us?

A. We must receive this blessing *by faith*; that is, we must *trust* in the righteousness of Christ as the only means of our pardon and acceptance.

CAN YOU TELL ME THEN,

Q. 33. What is justification?

Justification is an act of God's free grace, wherein he pardons all our sins, and accepts us as righteous in his sight only for the righteousness of Christ imputed to us, and received by faith alone.

Q. What is the next *act of God s free grace* or undeserved kindness?

A. It is *adoption*.

Q. What does *adoption* mean?

A. It means to take a poor stranger into one's family and treat him as a child belonging to the family, as a son or daughter.

Q. As spoken of in the Bible, what does the act of adoption do for us?

A. By it *we are received into the number of God s children*.

Q. What as such, are we entitled to?

A. We have *a right to all the privileges, or favors, of the sons of God*; we are treated as the good children of God.

THEREFORE,

Q. 34. What is adoption?

Adoption is an act of God's free grace, whereby we are received into the number, and have a right to all the privileges, of the sons of God.

OF SANCTIFICATION

Q. Is sanctification a *work*, or an *act of God's free grace*?

A. It is a *work* of God's free grace; it is not done in a moment, but continues during life and, like the other things just examined, shows the undeserved kindness of God.

Q. What change does this work produce in us?

A. By it *we are renewed in the whole man*; we are entirely changed for the better, in all the actings of our souls and bodies, in our thoughts, and feelings, and behavior.

Q. After whose image does this change take place?

A. *After the image of God*; that is, after his likeness, after his holiness and goodness.

Q. What are we thus enabled to do?

A. We are *enabled more and more to die unto sin*; that is, we become more and more disinclined and averse to sin.

Q. What else are we enabled to do, as the work of sanctification goes on?

A. We are enabled *more and more to live unto righteousness*; that is, we more readily and constantly do that which is right.

THEREFORE,

Q. 35. What is sanctification?

Sanctification is the work of God's free grace whereby we are renewed in the whole man after the image of God, and are enabled more and more to die unto sin and live unto righteousness.

BENEFITS FLOWING FROM JUSTIFICATION, ADOPTION, AND SANCTIFICATION

Q. What is the first benefit, or good, that is said to come from justification, adoption, and sanctification, *in this life*?

A. It is the *assurance of God s love*; or the being made sure that he loves us as his own children, who have begun to be holy, have begun to resemble him in our character, and to do his will.

Q. What is the next benefit arising from our being justified, adopted, and sanctified?

A. It is *peace of conscience*; peace of mind; the calm which arises from the idea of being in friendship with God, and of rendering obedience to him, or of doing what is right, what is pleasing to God.

Q. What is the next blessing?

A. It is *joy in the Holy Spirit*; that holy and happy state of mind which is produced by the Spirit. It takes place when we think of religious things and of our religious interests and hopes.

Q. What other benefit is to be considered?

A. The *increase of grace*.

Q. What does this mean?

A. It means an increase, or growth, in our love to God and to men. It means that we become more obedient to God's laws, and that we obey them with more and more pleasure.

Q. What other benefit is to be mentioned?

A. It is *perseverance in grace*; or the continuance through life in a course of piety and virtue; such a course as properly belongs to a Christian.

THEREFORE,

Q. 36. What are the benefits which in this life do accompany or flow from justification, adoption, and sanctification?

The benefits which, in this life, do accompany or flow from justification, adoption, and sanctification, are: assurance of

God's love, peace of conscience, joy in the Holy Spirit, increase of grace, and perseverance therein to the end.

BENEFITS OF REDEMPTION AT DEATH

Q. What are Christians called?

A. They are called *believers*, because they believe or trust in Christ as alone their Savior.

Q. What happy change takes place in the *souls of believers at death*?

A. Their souls *are made perfect in holiness*; they have no more wrong feelings, or desires, but all are as they should be, and such as to honor God and his holy law.

Q. Where do the souls of believers go at death?

A. They *do immediately pass into glory*; they are taken at once to heaven, where they receive all the honor and happiness they could desire.

Q. What becomes of their bodies?

A. Their *bodies do rest in their graves*, or remain in the ground, *until the resurrection*, the time when God designs to raise them to life again.

Q. During their rest in the ground are those bodies united to anything?

A. They are *united to Christ*. They are said to "sleep in Jesus," or to remain *in him*; that is, united to him, even in the grave. He regards their bodies as though connected with himself, and thus will not allow them to perish forever, but he will raise them to life again, to be always with him in glory.

THEREFORE,

Q. 37. What benefits do believers receive from Christ at death?

The souls of believers are at their death made perfect in holiness, and do immediately pass into glory, and their bodies, being still united to Christ, do rest in their graves till the resurrection.

BENEFITS OF REDEMPTION AT THE RESURRECTION

Q. What shall become of the bodies of believers *at the resurrection?*

A. They *shall be raised up in glory*; shall be raised to life, and in a far more excellent form and condition than in this life.

Q. What blessing shall be granted to believers in the day of judgment?

A. They *shall be openly acknowledged and acquitted at the day of judgment*; that is, shall be publicly owned as Christ's followers and friends, and declared to be forever free from punishment on account of past sins.

Q. Will believers receive any farther mark of God's favor?

A. They *shall be made perfectly blessed in the full enjoying of God to all eternity*; that is, they shall be altogether happy in the friendship and presence of God, not for a few years only, but forever.

THEREFORE,

Q. 38. What benefits do believers receive from Christ at the resurrection?

At the resurrection believers being raised up in glory, shall be openly acknowledged and acquitted in the day of judgment, and made perfectly blessed in the full enjoying of God to all eternity.

(Part Two: The Duty Which God Requires of Man)

NATURE OF MAN'S DUTY IN GENERAL

Q. What does God require of man?

A. He requires *duty*, or that which man owes to Him as being his creature, and his subject.

Q. Wherein has God set forth man's duty?

A. In his *revealed will*, or in the sacred Scriptures, which declare what it is God's wish and command that we should do and what we should refrain from doing.

Q. What does God require of man, in regard to his revealed will?

A. He requires *obedience* to it, and not simply the gaining a knowledge of it. He teaches us in the Scriptures what we are to do and to be, and expects us to act accordingly.

THEREFORE,

Q. 39. What is the duty which God requires of man?

The duty which God requires of man is obedience to his revealed will.

Q. Does God allow us to feel and act as we please?

A. No; he has given a *rule* to direct us.

Q. What is that rule called which he *at first revealed* or made known for *obedience*?

A. It is called the *moral law*; which means the rule of manners, or of duty.

THEREFORE,

Q. 40. What did God first reveal to man for the rule of his obedience?

The rule which God at first revealed to man for his obedience was the moral law.

SUMMARY OF THE MORAL LAW

Q. Is there any part of the Scriptures where our duty is expressed in few words?

A. Our duty, or the *moral law*, is expressed in few words in the *Ten Commandments*, and is therefore said to be *summarily comprehended* in them.

65

THEREFORE,

Q. 41. Wherein is the moral law summarily comprehended?

The moral law is summarily comprehended in the Ten Commandments.

THE SUM OF THE TEN COMMANDMENTS

Q. What one thing do the Ten Commandments require in substance?
A. The *sum*, or substance, of what they require is *love*.

Q. Whom do they require us to love?
A. *God, our neighbor, and ourselves.*

Q. How much do they require us to love God?
A. They require us to love God with all our powers, *with all our heart, with all our soul, with all our strength, and with all our mind.* We are to think more of God than of all other beings, and cheerfully to do all that he demands of us.

Q. How much may and should we love our neighbor?

A. We should love *our neighbor as ourselves*; look upon him with the same kind of interest, and promote his welfare.

Q. Who is our *neighbor*?
A. Any and every human being is our neighbor; especially those whom we may reach by our kindness.

Q. How much may we love *ourselves*?
A. Far less than we love God, for we are infinitely less worthy of love and attention than he.

Q. How shall we know when we love God more than we love ourselves?
A. When we care more and try more to do his will than our own, to please him more than ourselves. We should ask him daily, "Lord what will you have me to do?"

Q. What should we ask concerning our fellow-men?
A. We should inquire of ourselves, how can I be useful to my fellow-men today? What do they need, and how can I serve them, and make them happier than they are?

Q. When do we love our neighbor as ourselves?
A. When we do to others as we think they ought to do to us, if we were placed as they are.

THEREFORE,

Q. 42. What is the sum of the Ten Commandments?

The sum of the Ten Commandments is to love the Lord our God with all our heart, with all our soul, with all our strength, and with all our mind; and our neighbor as ourselves.

PREFACE TO THE TEN COMMANDMENTS

Q. What is that part called which goes before the Ten Commandments?
A. It is called the *preface*.

Q. Where had the Israelites lived before the Ten Commandments were given to them?
A. In the land of Egypt.

Q. What is that land called in the preface?
A. It is called the *house of bondage*; because, while in that land, the Israelites were slaves to the Egyptians.

THEREFORE,

Q. 43. What is the preface to the Ten Commandments?

The preface to the Ten Commandments is in these words, "I am the Lord thy God, which have brought you out of the land of Egypt, out of the house of bondage."

Q. What is said of God in this preface?

A. He is said to be *the Lord, and our God, and Redeemer.*

Q. What is meant by these expressions?

A. They teach us that God is the highest and greatest Being, that he has been to us the kindest Being, and ever will be, and that he has shown his love by sending his Son to redeem or deliver us from sin and from everlasting pain.

Q. Since God is so great and good a Being, what is due from us to him?

A. It is plain that *we are bound to keep all his commandments.*

THEREFORE,

Q. 44. What does the preface to the Ten Commandments teach us?

The preface to the Ten Commandments teaches us that because God is the Lord, and our God and Redeemer, therefore we are bound to keep all his commandments.

THE FIRST COMMANDMENT

Q. What is it to *have a god*?
A. It is to place our love and to depend on some being or thing more strongly than on any other being or thing.

Q. Does God care anything about what we love, or depend upon?
A. Yes; he is very particular and exact about this matter, as we learn from the first commandment.

THEREFORE,

Q. 45. What is the first commandment?

The first commandment is, You shall have no other gods before me.

Q. Does God care whether we *know* or become acquainted with him; whether we *acknowledge* or admit that he is *the only true God*?

A. He requires us thus to know and acknowledge him to be the only true, the only real and living God.

Q. Does he require us to do anything more?

A. He requires us to think of him, and to consider him as *our God, and to worship and glorify* (or honor) *him accordingly*; that is, as our God and the only true God.

THEREFORE,

Q. 46. What is required in the first commandment?

The first commandment requires us to know and acknowledge God to be the only true God, and our God; and to worship and glorify him accordingly.

Q. What is meant by the *denying of God*?

A. It means to deny that there is a God; or it is to think or say that there is no God.

71

Q. Are we at liberty *not to* worship and glorify the true God as our God?

A. God will be offended greatly with us if we do not worship and honor him as *our God*, as the Being whom we most love and respect.

Q. What other thing will greatly offend him?

A. The *giving of that worship and glory* (or honor) *to any other being, which is due to him alone*, or which he alone is worthy of.

THEREFORE,

Q. 47. What is forbidden in the first commandment?

The first commandment forbids the denying or not worshiping and glorifying the true God as God and our God, and the giving of that worship and glory to any other which is due to him alone.

Q. If we honor and love any other than the true God, will he know the fact?

A. He will; for *he seeks all things* that are done, and *takes notice* of them, looks at them closely, and especially if they ought not to be done.

Q. What is that which greatly displeases him?
A. He is *much displeased with the sin of having any other God.*

Q. What sin is that?
A. The sin of loving and honoring any being besides himself, as the best or most worthy, and the best suited to make us happy.

THEREFORE,

Q. 48. What are we especially taught by the words [*before me*] in the first commandment?

These words [before me] in the first commandment teach us, that God, who sees all things, takes notice of, and is much displeased with the sin of having any other God.

THE SECOND COMMANDMENT

Q. What is a *graven image*?

73

A. It is something cut out of wood, or stone, or metal, in the form or *likeness* of some being; and made for the purpose of being worshiped and honored as sacred or divine.

Q. How is worship to such an image usually expressed?
A. By the act of *praying to* and *bowing down* before it, and thus showing that we consider it better and higher than ourselves.

Q. What is meant when it is said that God is *jealous*?
A. It means that he cannot bear that any being or thing should have so much love and service as ought to be given to him.

Q. How has he shown his displeasure at those who love other things more than himself?
A. He has shown it by making the children of such persons suffer on their account.

Q. What is this act of God called?
A. It is called the *visiting the iniquity of the fathers upon the children*.

Q. How far is this carried?
A. *Unto the third and fourth generation*; that is, to the grandchildren and great-grandchildren.

Q. What is the character of those whose iniquity is thus punished?

A. They are those *who hate God.*

Q. How does God treat those who love him?
A. He *shows mercy unto thousands of them that love him, and keep his commandments.*

THEREFORE,

Q. 49. What is the second commandment?

The second commandment is, You shall not make any graven image, or any likeness of anything that is in heaven above, or that is in the earth beneath, or that is in the water under the earth. You shall not bow down to them, nor serve them; for I, the Lord your God, am a jealous God, visiting the iniquity of the fathers upon the children, unto the third and fourth generation of them that hate me; and showing mercy unto thousands of them that love me and keep my commandments.

Q. What has God appointed, or ordered, in his word?
A. In *his word* (the Scriptures) God *has appointed,* or required us to observe *religious worship and ordinances.*

Q. What is meant by *religious ordinances*?

A. They are certain means or ways by which God is honored; such as prayers, singing God's praises, baptism, the Lord's Supper, and the Sabbath.

Q. Concerning this religious worship and ordinances, what does he require?

A. He commands the *receiving, observing, and keeping them pure and entire*. That is, he commands them to be attended to as he first made them known; without our adding to, or taking from them, or altering their form and intention.

THEREFORE,

Q. 50. What is required in the second commandment?

The second commandment requires the receiving, observing, and keeping pure and entire, all such religious worship and ordinances as God hath appointed in his word.

Q. What wrong way is there of worshiping God?

A. By means of *images*, carved, or painted, likenesses of anything in nature, or of God himself.

Q. 51. What is forbidden in the second commandment?

The second commandment forbids the worshiping of God by images, or any other way not appointed by his word.

Q. What is meant by the words, *God's sovereignty over us*?
A. They mean the fact that God is *the Lord*, the highest Being, and altogether above us, and has the best right to command us as to what we are to do and to be.

Q. What do we mean when we speak of *God's propriety in us*?
A. We mean that he has a right to dispose of us as he pleases; that we are his property, being his creatures; and, moreover, that he has bought us with the blood of his Son as our Redeemer.

Q. Has God a strong desire to be worshiped in those very ways which he has marked out in the Bible?
A. He has great *zeal*, a warm concern, in reference *to his own worship*.

Q. 52. What are the reasons annexed (or joined) to the second commandment?

The reasons annexed to the second commandment are, God's sovereignty over us, his propriety in us, and the zeal he has to his own worship.

THE THIRD COMMANDMENT

Q. What is meant by the *name of the Lord*?
A. Any word, or expression, by which he has taught us to call him; or which he applies to himself in the Bible.

Q. What is it *to take the name of God in vain*?
A. It is to think or speak of any of his names in an unworthy, irreligious, or common manner.

Q. What will he do to the person who thus treats his name?
A. He *will not hold him guiltless*; he will hold him liable to be punished; he will severely punish him.

THEREFORE,

Q. 53. What is the third commandment?

The third commandment is, You shall not take the name of the Lord your God in vain; for the Lord will not hold him guiltless that takes his name in vain.

Q. What sort of *use* may we make of *God s names*?
A. None but a *holy and reverent use*; we are to think of them as sacred, and worthy of the highest respect; we are not to be careless and familiar with them, as with the names of creatures.

Q. Is there anything relating to God, beside his names, which we are bound to use in a serious and most respectful manner?
A. We are so to use his *titles*; his titles, for instance, as "The God of heaven," or "The Holy One of Israel," and so on.

Q. And what else, relating to God, must we revere?
A. His *attributes*, the qualities that belong to him; his goodness, justice, truth, and holiness, among all others.

Q. And is there not something else, pertaining to God, which is to be treated with great respect and reverence?

A. Yes; his *ordinances* (baptism and the Lord's Supper), his *word* (the Bible), and *works* (those of creation, providence, and redemption).

THEREFORE,

Q. 54. What is required in the third commandment?

The third commandment requires the holy and reverent use of God's names, titles, attributes, ordinances, word, and works.

Q. What does God forbid in this commandment?
A. He forbids the *profaning of anything by which he makes himself known*; he forbids it to be used in a gross, bold, thoughtless, dishonorable manner.

Q. What may such *profaning* of what relates to God be called?
A. It may be called the *abusing* of it; that is, it is the opposite of a proper and becoming use of what relates to God.

THEREFORE,

Q. 55. What is forbidden in the third commandment?

The third commandment forbids all profaning or abusing of anything whereby God makes himself known.

Q. Will those who break the third commandment *escape punishment?*

A. They may escape punishment from men, yet God will not, suffer them to go unpunished; they must expect *his righteous judgment*; that is, a punishment according to his just sentence or decision against them.

THEREFORE,

Q. 56. What is the reason annexed to the third commandment?

The reason annexed to the third commandment is, that however the breakers of this commandment may escape punishment from men, yet the Lord our God will not suffer them to escape his righteous judgment.

81

Q. What is the best day of the week?

A. The Sabbath-day.

Q. Why is it the best?

A. Because it is to be *kept holy*, or spent in a religious manner.

Q. Is it lawful to work on that day?

A. It is not lawful; it was designed for no such purpose.

Q. How many days of the week are given us in which our worldly business is to be done?

A. *Six days* are allowed us for that.

Q. What did God do in six days, a long time since?

A. *In six days the Lord made heaven, and earth, the sea, and all that in them is.*

Q. After the six days of work, what did God do?

A. On the seventh day *he rested*; that is, he did not work, he refrained from creating any more things at that time.

Q. Did the Lord, on this account, require any difference to be made between the Sabbath-day and the other days of the week?

A. He *blessed the Sabbath-day and hallowed it*; he pronounced it a day which he would make most useful to man, and a day in which God should especially be worshiped.

THEREFORE,

Q. 57. Which is the fourth commandment?

The fourth commandment is, Remember the Sabbath-day, to keep it holy. Six days shall you labor, and do all your work; but the seventh day is the Sabbath of the Lord your God: in it you shall not do any work; you, nor your son, nor your daughter, your man-servant, nor your maid-servant, nor your cattle, nor your stranger that is within your gates. For in six days the Lord made heaven and earth, the sea, and all that in them is, and rested the seventh day, wherefore the Lord blessed the Sabbath-day, and hallowed it.

Q. Has God directed us to *keep holy*, or to set apart, any particular time for religious duties?
A. He has directed, in the Scriptures, *set*, or stated and regular *times* to be used in this way.

Q. Has he required one whole day in every seven days?
A. He has *expressly*, or plainly, so required.

83

Q. 58. What is required in the fourth commandment?

The fourth commandment requires the keeping holy to God such set times as he has appointed in his Word, expressly one whole day in seven, to be a holy Sabbath to himself.

CHANGE OF THE SABBATH

Q. For how long a time was the *seventh day of the week* (our Saturday) to be observed as the *weekly Sabbath*, or day of holy rest?

A. *From the beginning of the world to the resurrection of Christ*, God appointed or required the seventh day to be spent in a holy and religious manner.

Q. After Christ rose from the dead, what other day became sacred in place of the seventh?

A. The *first day of the week* then became the religious day, and *ever since* has been, and is to *continue to the end of the world*, and is the *Christian Sabbath*, the day to be observed by all Christians, and in honor of Christ their only Savior.

Q. 59. Which day of the seven has God appointed to be the weekly Sabbath?

From the beginning of the world to the resurrection of Christ, God appointed the seventh day of the week to be the weekly Sabbath, and the first day of the week ever since, to continue to the end of the world; which is the Christian Sabbath.

THE SANCTIFICATION OF THE SABBATH

Q. What is the *sanctifying of the Sabbath*?
A. It is to use or spend it in a holy, or religious manner.

Q. How is this done?
A. By *laying aside on that day all common business and all sports and pleasures*, even such as are *proper on other days*.

Q. Is it enough simply to avoid these things on the Sabbath?
A. By no means: we are bound also to attend to religious duties, and to *spend the whole time in worshiping God publicly and privately* (at church or at home); except so much as may be required for *works that cannot be done at*

another time, and works needful to relieve the sick, the miserable, and tits helpless.

Q. 60. How is the Sabbath to be sanctified?

The Sabbath is to be sanctified by a holy resting all that day, even from such worldly employments and recreations as are lawful on other days; and spending the whole time in the public and private exercises of God's worship, except so much as is to be taken up in the works of necessity and mercy.

Q. As to the duties of the Sabbath, what does God forbid?
A. God forbids the *omission*, that is, the not doing of the duties required; and he also forbids their *careless performance*, that is, the doing of them in a thoughtless and unsuitable manner.

Q. What else does God forbid, in relation to the Sabbath?
A. He forbids *the profaning the day by idleness*, and the *doing of that which is in itself sinful.*

Q. Does he forbid anything else about this matter?

A. God forbids *unnecessary thoughts, words, or works, about our worldly employments or recreations.*

Q. What does this mean?
A. He forbids us to think, speak, or act in a worldly manner, on the Sabbath, except so far as it cannot be avoided.

ON THE WHOLE THEN,

Q. 61. What is forbidden in the fourth commandment?

The fourth commandment forbids the omission or careless performance of the duties required, and the profaning the day by idleness, or doing that which is in itself sinful, or by unnecessary thoughts, words, or works, about our worldly employments and recreations.

Q. What is the *first reason* stated for keeping the Sabbath in a religious manner?
A. *God's allowing us six days of the week for our employments,* or business.

Q. What is the *second reason*?

A. *His challenging a special propriety in the seventh*; that is, his claiming that that day especially belongs to him, and is to be spent in honor of him.

Q. What is the *third reason* for keeping the Sabbath as a day of sacred rest?
A. God's *own example*; he refrained on that day from the work of creating, which he had been performing on the other six days of the week.

Q. What is the *fourth reason*?
A. *His blessing the seventh day*; his declaring it to be a day for man's religious welfare.

HENCE,

Q. 62. What are the reasons annexed to the fourth commandment?

The reasons annexed to the fourth commandment are, God's allowing us six days of the week for our own employments; his challenging a special propriety in the seventh; his own example; and his blessing the Sabbath-day.

Q. Whom does God require us to honor?

A. He says, *honor thy father and thy mother*.

Q. How is this to be done?

A. We must think highly of them, do what they wish us to do, and support them, if we can, should they be poor.

Q. Is there any reward promised for such conduct toward our parents?

A. To the command he adds, *That your days may be long in the land which the Lord your God gives you*.

Q. What *land* is here spoken of?

A. The land of Canaan, or Judea, toward which the Israelites were journeying when the law was given at Sinai.

THEREFORE,

Q. 63. Which is the fifth commandment?

The fifth commandment is, Honor your father and your mother, that your days may be long upon the land which the Lord your God gives you.

Q. Is *honor* to be shown to any beside our parents?

A. Yes; to other *superiors*, to *inferiors*, and to *equals*.

Q. Who are intended by *superiors*?

A. Those who are above us, or hold a more important place; such as our parents, rulers, masters, teachers, etc.

Q. Who are meant by *inferiors*?

A. By such are intended children, subjects, apprentices, pupils, etc.

Q. And who are meant by *equals?*

A. Those that are of the same rank and standing with ourselves; our brothers, sisters, school-mates, and neighbors of the same classes.

Q. What are we to do with all such?

A. We are to *preserve the honor* due to such, and *perform the duties* which we owe to them.

THEREFORE,

Q. 64. What is required in the fifth commandment?

The fifth commandment requires the preserving the honor and performing the duties belonging to everyone in their several places and relations, as superiors, inferiors, or equals.

Q. Is it proper to *neglect the honor and duty* which we owe other persons?

A. God forbids the *neglecting of the honor* due to them. That is, he forbids the not giving to them the respect and service which they ought to receive.

Q. Are we allowed to do anything against the honor and duty belonging to them?

A. God forbids the *doing anything against the honor*, or respect, or *duty*, which belongs to persons in different situations in life.

THEREFORE,

Q. 65. What is forbidden in the fifth commandment?

The fifth commandment forbids the neglecting of, or doing anything against, the honor and duty which belongs to everyone, in their several places, and relations.

Q. Is there any particular *reason annexed*, or joined to the fifth commandment, to induce us to keep it?

A. There is a *promise of long life and prosperity to all such as keep this commandment.*

Q. What is meant by a life of prosperity?

A. A happy life; one in which God shows to us special kindness.

Q. Do all who keep the fifth commandment live a long life, and do they have an uncommon share of earthly blessings?

A. They have as long and as prosperous a life as shall be *for the glory*, or honor, *of God*, and *for their own good*. That is, God causes them to live in this world as long, and to have as many good things, as he thinks best both for himself and for them, and that is all that we should desire.

THEREFORE,

Q. 66. What is the reason annexed to the fifth commandment?

The reason annexed to the fifth commandment, is a promise of long life and prosperity (as far as it shall serve for God's glory and their own good) to all such as keep this commandment.

THE SIXTH COMMANDMENT

Q. 67. What is the sixth commandment?

The sixth commandment is, You shall not kill.

Q. To whom does this commandment relate?

A. To human beings, not to the lower animals.

Q. Are we only bound *not* to destroy human life?

A. We are required to *preserve our own life and the life of others.*

Q. How are we to do this?

A. Only by such *endeavors*, or acts, as the law of God allows.

THEREFORE,

Q. 68. What is required in the sixth commandment?

The sixth commandment requires all lawful endeavors to preserve our own life, and the life of others.

Q. Is the life of our neighbor, or fellow-man, to be cared for as well as our own?

A. It is to be looked upon as of great value; and so is our own life to be regarded,

Q. Have we any right to take away our own life?

A. We have no right to take away our own life; God reserves that right to himself.

Q. Does God forbid us to take the life of our neighbor?

A. He forbids *the taking away of the life of our neighbor unjustly*; that is, without good and sufficient reason.

Q. May it ever justly be taken away?

A. It may justly be taken away, as a punishment for certain great crimes, or in defending our own lives when we are unjustly attacked.

Q. By whom is life to be taken away for crime?

A. Only by the proper officers of justice, appointed by government; and according to the forms required by law.

Q. Does God forbid the doing of what tends to destroy or shorten life?

A. God forbids *whatsoever tends thereunto.*

Q. 69. What is forbidden in the sixth commandment?

The sixth commandment forbids the taking away of our own life, or the life of our neighbor unjustly, or whatsoever tends thereunto.

THE SEVENTH COMMANDMENT

Q. 70. Which is the seventh commandment?

The seventh commandment is, You shall not commit adultery.

Q. What are we required to preserve, or keep?

A. We are required to *preserve our own and our neighbor s chastity*, or modesty and purity.

Q. In what particulars is chastity to be preserved?

A. We are required to be chaste, or modest, *in heart, speech, and behavior*; that is, in our thoughts and desires; in our words; and in our looks and other actions.

THEREFORE,

Q. 71. What is required in the seventh commandment?

The seventh commandment requires the preservation of our own and our neighbor's chastity, in heart, speech, and behavior.

Q. What vicious thoughts, words, and actions are forbidden?

A. Those which are *unchaste*, immodest, and corrupting.

THEREFORE,

Q. 72. What is forbidden in the seventh commandment?

The seventh commandment forbids all unchaste thoughts, words, and actions.

THE EIGHTH COMMANDMENT

Q. May we take and use as our own that which belongs to other persons?
A. We may not; for it is against the eighth commandment to do so.

THEREFORE,

Q. 73. Which is the eight commandment?

The eighth commandment is, You shall not steal.

Q. How are we to procure *outward estate*, or property?
A. Only in a *lawful* and proper manner.

Q. How are we *to further*, or increase *the wealth and outward estate of ourselves and others*?
A. Only in such methods as are *lawful*; such as the law of God allows.

THEREFORE,

Q. 74. What is required in the eighth commandment?

The eighth commandment requires the lawful procuring and furthering the wealth and outward estate of ourselves and others.

Q. Is it right to neglect our temporal welfare and estate?
A. God *forbids whatsoever does or may unjustly hinder our own wealth and outward estate.*

Q. Are we to have any care for the interests of our neighbor?
A. God forbids our doing anything that may wrongly hinder *our neighbor's wealth and outward estate.*

THEREFORE,

Q. 75. What is forbidden in the eight commandment?

The eighth commandment forbids whatsoever does or may unjustly hinder our own, or our neighbor's wealth or outward estate.

THE NINTH COMMANDMENT

Q. What sort of *witness*, or testimony, are we not to *bear against our neighbor*?

A. *False* witness. We are to say nothing against him that is not true.

THEREFORE,

Q. 76. Which is the ninth commandment?

The ninth commandment is, You shall not bear false witness against your neighbor.

Q. What are we to maintain and promote between man and man?

A. God requires the *maintaining and promoting of truth*; that is, he requires us, when speaking of any person, to state the exact truth, and to induce others to do the same.

Q. What does God require concerning the *good name* of ourselves and others?

A. He requires the preservation and improvement of that good name, or respectful regard, among men.

Q. When are we to be particularly careful to speak the truth, and to care for the good name, or reputation of others?

A. When we speak under oath, as *witnesses* in a court of justice.

THEREFORE,

Q. 77. What is required in the ninth commandment?

The ninth commandment requires the maintaining and promoting of truth between man and man, and of our own and our neighbor's good name, especially in witness-bearing.

Q. When is a thing *prejudicial to truth*?

A. When it is *hurtful* to truth; when it gives us a wrong opinion of any person's conduct or character.

THEREFORE,

Q. 78. What is forbidden in the ninth commandment?

The ninth commandment forbids whatsoever is prejudicial to truth, or injurious to our own or our neighbor's good name.

THE TENTH COMMANDMENT

Q. *To covet* anything; what is meant by the phrase?
A. It means to desire to gain or to obtain that thing.

Q. What does this state of mind arise from?
A. It arises from a want of contentment with our present lot; for if we are contented with what we have, we shall not be likely to desire what belongs to another man.

Q. What thought is calculated to make us contented?
A. That that condition of life is best for us which God seems to have placed us in.

THEREFORE,

Q. 79. Which is the tenth commandment?

The tenth commandment is, You shall not covet your neighbor's house; you shall not covet your neighbor's wife, nor his man-servant, nor his maidservant, nor his ox, nor his donkey, nor any thing that is your neighbor's.

Q. What is meant by the word *contentment*?
A. It means an easy and quiet state of mind; the being satisfied with such things as God has given us.

Q. What is to be the proper feeling toward our neighbors?
A. *A right and charitable frame of spirit*; that is, a kind and loving temper; a desire that others may be happy, as well as ourselves; and that everything belonging to them may do well.

THEREFORE,

Q. 80. What is required in the tenth commandment?

The tenth commandment requires full contentment with our own condition; with a right and charitable frame of spirit toward our neighbor, and all that is his.

Q. With what are we not to be *discontented*, or uneasy?

A. *With our own estate,* or situation in life.

Q. What are we not to envy, or grieve at, or be unhappy for?

A. We are not to be uneasy and unhappy in view of the *good of our neighbor*, or of his welfare in any respect.

Q. Respecting our neighbor's property, what does God forbid?

A. God forbids *all inordinate motions and affections to anything that is his*; that is, all unreasonable desires and wishes, and purposes to obtain what belongs to our neighbor.

THEREFORE,

Q. 81. What is forbidden in the tenth commandment?

The tenth commandment forbids all discontentment with our own estate, envying or grieving at the good of our neighbor, and all inordinate motions and affections to anything that is his.

SPECIAL DUTIES WHICH GOD REQUIRES OF MAN UNDER THE GOSPEL DISPENSATION

Man s inability to keep the Law.

Q. What is man not able to do?

A. *No mere man is able perfectly to keep the commandments of God.*

Q. During what time is he not able?

A. *In this life.*

Q. How long is it since man was able to keep them?

A. *Since the fall*, or the first sin of Adam.

Q. How often does he break God's commandments?

A. *Daily.*

Q. How does he break them?

A. *In thought, word, and deed.*

Q. What man, and yet not a *mere man*, did always perfectly keep the commandments of God?

A. Jesus Christ, who was God as well as man.

THEREFORE,

Q. 82. Is any man able perfectly to keep the commandment of God?

No mere man since the fall is able in this life perfectly to keep the commandments of God, but breaks them daily in thought, word, and deed.

DIFFERENT DEGREES OF GUILT

Q. How do sins appear *in the sight of God*?
A. They appear *heinous*, hateful, bad.

Q. Do all sins seem to God alike heinous?
A. *Some sins in themselves are more heinous*, or bad, than others.

Q. What makes some sins more heinous than other sins?
A. Some sins are more heinous than others, *by reason of several aggravations* which belong to them; that is, on account of several things connected with them that make them worse than otherwise they would have been.

THEREFORE,

Q. 83. Are all transgressions of the law equally heinous?

Some sins in themselves, and by reason of several aggravations, are more heinous in the sight of God than others.

WHAT SIN DESERVES

Q. What does every sin deserve?
A. *Every sin deserves God's wrath and curse*; his displeasure, and the punishment that shows his displeasure.

Q. How long, and where, does sin deserve these?
A. *Both in this life, and that which is to come.*

Q. How long is the life to come?
A. It is everlasting.

Q. How long a punishment then do we deserve for every sin, for every instance in which we do what God forbids, or fail to do what God requires?
A. We deserve everlasting punishment.

THEREFORE,

Q. 84. What does every sin deserve?

Every sin deserves God's wrath and curse, both in this life and that which is to come.

SPECIAL DUTIES

Q. What is *due to us for sin*?
A. *The wrath and curse of God.*

Q. To *escape* this, what does God require?
A. *God requires faith in Jesus Christ.*

Q. Is that all?
A. He requires, also, *repentance unto life*, that change of mind and conduct which leads to *life*, or happiness.

Q. What does God require besides these?
A. They are to be followed *with a diligent* (or earnest) *use of all the outward means* of religion.

Q. What means are these?
A. Those *whereby Christ communicates* (or giveth) *to us the benefits of redemption.*

Q. What are the benefits of redemption?
A. The blessings purchased by the blood of Christ are given to us on account of his death.

Q. 85. What does God require of us that we may escape his wrath and curse due to us for sin?

To escape the wrath and curse of God due to us for sin, God requires of us faith in Jesus Christ, repentance unto life, with the diligent use of all the outward means whereby Christ communicates to us the benefits of redemption.

FAITH IN CHRIST

Q. In whom are we to *have faith*?
A. We are to have *faith in Jesus Christ*.

Q. What is this thing?
A. It *is a saving grace*; or *a favor* which God grants, as necessary to our being saved from sin and from hell.

Q. What sort of a thing is faith?
A. It is that state of our mind and feelings *whereby we receive Christ*, regard him, and *rest upon him alone*, depend on him alone, *for salvation*.

Q. How are we to receive and to rest upon him?

A. *As he is offered*, or presented to us, *in the Gospel*; in the New Testament.

Q. How is he offered therein?
A. As a prophet, priest, and king (see questions 23-26).

T H E R E F O R E ,

Q. 86. What is faith in Jesus Christ?

Faith in Jesus Christ is a saving grace, whereby we receive and rest upon him alone for salvation, as he is offered to us in the Gospel.

REPENTANCE

Q. What other *saving grace* is there besides faith?
A. *Repentance unto life.*

Q. What is this *grace*, or favor?
A. It is that *whereby a sinner turns from his sin unto God.*

Q. With what purpose and intention?
A. *With full purpose of new obedience*, or of a new and better manner of life.

Q. With what besides such a purpose?

A. *With endeavor after new obedience*; he tries hard to live the new life he has purposed or determined to follow.

Q. What led him thus to turn from his sin?

A. He did it *out of a true sense of his sin*; from a deep feeling that he had done wrong, had done wickedly in sinning against God.

Q. What besides this led him to turn?

A. It was an *apprehension of the mercy of God in Christ*; a laying hold of the mercy which God offers to sinners on account of Christ, arising from a clear idea of that mercy.

Q. What feelings are produced by this true sense of sin and believing view of divine mercy?

A. *Grief and hatred of sin* are thereby produced.

THEREFORE,

Q. 87. What is repentance unto life?

Repentance unto life is a saving grace, whereby a sinner, out of a true sense of his sin, and apprehension of the mercy of God in Christ, does, with grief and hatred of his sin, turn from it unto God, with full purpose of, and endeavor after new obedience.

THE OUTWARD MEANS OF SALVATION

Q. What *benefits*, or blessings, does Christ *communicate*, or bestow?
A. *Christ communicates to us the benefits of redemption.*

Q. By what *outward and ordinary means*?
A. By *his ordinances*; that is, by certain things which God has appointed to be attended to, in order to obtain salvation.

Q. What are the principal outward means of salvation?
A. They are the *Word*, *Sacraments*, and *Prayer*.

Q. To what persons are they *made effectual*?
A. *All* these means are *made effectual to the elect for salvation*; that is, in the use of them the elect are saved.

THEREFORE,

Q. 88. What are the outward and ordinary means whereby Christ communicates to us the benefits of redemption?

The outward and ordinary means whereby Christ communicates to us the benefits of redemption, are his ordinances, especially the Word, sacraments, and prayer; all which are made effectual to the elect for salvation.

EFFECTS OF THE WORD OF GOD

Q. What does the Spirit of God make of the reading, but especially of the preaching of the Word?

A. *He makes them an effectual means of convincing and converting sinners.*

Q. Of what does the Word of God *convince* sinners?

A. It convinces them of their being sinners, and as such exposed to destruction, and therefore needing salvation.

Q. What is meant by *converting* sinners?

A. It is turning, or changing, their feelings from the hatred of God and holiness to the love of both.

Q. After sinners are converted, what does the Spirit of God do for them?

A. He makes the Word a means of *building them up in holiness and comfort unto salvation*; that is, of making them more holy and happy.

Q. How is this done?

A. *Through faith* on their part; by causing them to *believe, and trust in,* what the Word of God declares.

THEREFORE,

Q. 89. How is the Word made effectual to salvation?

The Spirit of God makes the reading, but especially the preaching of the Word an effectual means of convincing and converting sinners, and of building them up in holiness and comfort, through faith, unto salvation.

PROPER USE OF THE WORD OF GOD

Q. *That the Word may become effectual to salvation,* what must we do?

A. *We must attend thereunto with diligence, preparation, and prayer;* we must put ourselves in a right state of mind; that is, we must think seriously of what we read or hear of the Word of God—and we must pray about it.

Q. Is there anything else to be done?
A. We must *receive it with faith and love.*

Q. Is that all?

A. We must *lay it up in our hearts, and practice it in our lives*; that is, we must remember, regard, and do what the Bible teaches us, if we would be saved.

THEREFORE,

Q. 90. How is the Word to be read and heard, that it may become effectual to salvation?

That the Word may become effectual to salvation, we must attend thereunto with diligence, preparation, and prayer, receive it with faith, and love, lay it up in our hearts, and practice it in our lives.

THE EFFICACY OF THE SACRAMENTS

Q. What do the sacraments become?

A. *The sacraments become effectual means of saltation.*

Q. How do they so become?

A. *Not from any virtue in them, or in him that administers them*; that is, not from any power in the sacraments, or in the minister.

Q. How then do they become *effectual*, or powerful?

A. *Only by the blessing of Christ*; by the power which he gives them over our feelings.

Q. What is added to the blessing of Christ?

A. *The working of his Spirit in them that by faith receive them*; that is, receive the sacraments.

THEREFORE,

Q. 91. How do the sacraments become effectual means of salvation?

The sacraments become effectual means of salvation, not from any virtue in them or in him that administers them; but only by the blessing of Christ, and the working of his Spirit in them that by faith receive them.

OF THE NATURE OF THE SACRAMENTS

Q. What do you mean by a sacrament?

A. *A sacrament is a holy ordinance*, or outward form of religion.

Q. By whom was it *instituted*, or commanded?

A. It was *instituted by Christ*.

Q. What is it intended to show forth?

A. *Christ, and the benefits of the New Covenant*, or the blessings of the Gospel.

Q. How is this done?

A. *By sensible signs*: by things that we can perceive; by our *senses*; by the eye, taste, touch, etc.

Q. In a sacrament, what is done with respect to *Christ and the benefits of the New Covenant*?

A. They are therein *represented, sealed, and applied to believers*.

Q. How are they *represented*?

A. They are therein set forth in a striking manner.

Q. What is meant by their being *sealed?*

A. They are *made sure* to us.

Q. What further is done?

A. They are *applied* (that is, given) *to believers*; to those who trust in Christ.

THEREFORE,

Q. 92. What is a sacrament?

A sacrament is a holy ordinance instituted by Christ; wherein, by sensible signs, Christ, and the benefits of the new covenant, are represented, sealed, and applied to believers.

THE SACRAMENTS OF THE NEW TESTAMENT

Q. 93. Which are the Sacraments of the New Testament?

The sacraments of the New Testament are baptism and the Lord's Supper.

OF THE NATURE AND USE OF BAPTISM

Q. What is the *sensible sign* used in baptism?
A. It is *water*.

Q. What is done with the water?
A. There is a *washing with water*.

Q. In whose name is water put upon the baptized person?
A. *In the name of the Father, and of the Son, and of the Holy Spirit.*

Q. What does this *washing with water signify and seal*?

A. It does *signify and seal our ingrafting into Christ*; that is, our being united to Christ, our being Christians.

Q. What else does it signify and seal?

A. It does signify and seal our *partaking of the benefits of the covenant of grace*; the blessings offered to believers in the Gospel.

Q. Of what else is it a sign and seal?

A. It signifies *our engagement to be the Lord s*; our duty and choice to be given up entirely to the service of Christ, and to be treated according to his will.

THEREFORE,

Q. 94. What is baptism?

Baptism is a sacrament, wherein the washing with water, in the name of the Father, and of the Son, and of the Holy Spirit signifies and seal our ingrafting into Christ, and partaking of the benefits of the covenant of grace, and our engagement to be the Lord's.

Q. To whom is baptism *not* to be administered?

A. *Baptism is not to be administered* (or given) *to any that are out of the visible Church*; that is, have not professed to be Christians and joined the Church now *seen* on earth.

Q. Is baptism never to be given to such?

A. Not *till they profess their faith in Christ and obedience to him.*

Q. Is anything said concerning their infant children?

A. *The infants of such as are members of the visible Church are to be baptized.*

THEREFORE,

Q. 95. To whom is baptism to be administered?

Baptism is not to be administered to any that are out of the visible Church, till they profess their faith in Christ, and obedience to him; but the infants of such as are members of the visible Church are to be baptized.

OF THE NATURE AND USE OF THE LORD'S SUPPER

Q. What are the *sensible signs* used in the sacrament of the Lord's Supper?

A. *Bread and wine.*

Q. Why are they used?

A. It is *according to Christ's appointment*, or direction.

Q. For what purpose, and how, are they used?

A. *By giving and receiving bread and wine, his death is showed forth*; there is here something strongly to remind us of his painful death.

Q. Who are *made partakers of his body and blood*?

A. *The worthy receivers*; those who receive the Lord's Supper in a right manner.

Q. How are the worthy receivers made partakers of his body and blood?

A. *Not after a corporal and carnal manner, but by faith*; that is, not by eating and drinking simply, but by eating and drinking in the exercise of *faith*; having their thoughts and feelings engaged about Christ and the blessings which he promises.

Q. To be *made partakers of Christ's body and blood*, what is intended?

A. It means to be partakers of the blessings procured by his body broken and his blood shed.

Q. Hence, what is added?

A. The worthy receivers are said to be partakers of his body and blood, *with all his benefits*.

Q. And what is the advantage to them of observing this sacrament?

A. It is to their *spiritual nourishment* (or strength) and to their *growth in grace*. Its effect is to make them stronger, and better, and happier Christians.

THEREFORE,

Q. 96. What is the Lord's Supper?

The Lord's Supper is a sacrament, wherein, by giving and receiving bread and wine, according to Christ's appointment, his death is showed forth; and the worthy receivers are, not after a corporal and carnal manner, but by faith, made partakers of his body and blood, with all his benefits, to their spiritual nourishment, and growth in grace.

OF THE PROPER OBSERVANCE OF THE
LORD'S SUPPER

Q. What is *required of them that would worthily*, or in a suitable manner, *partake of the Lord's Supper*?

A. It is required of them, *that they examine themselves of their knowledge to discern the Lord's body*; that they ask whether they understand that the bread and wine are designed to remind them of Christ and of his sufferings.

Q. Concerning what other things must they examine themselves?

A. *Of their faith to feed upon him*; that is, whether they so believe and trust in Christ, herein set forth, that in partaking of the bread and wine, they derive from Christ the blessings which he died to procure for them.

Q. Are there not some other things concerning which they must examine or try themselves?

A. *Of their repentance, love, and new obedience.*

Q. Why should they try themselves on all these points?

A. *Lest, coming unworthily, they eat and drink judgment to themselves.*

Q. What is meant by coming unworthily?

A. Coming in an ignorant, careless, and improper state of mind, and while living in an unchristian manner.

Q. What is meant by eating and drinking *judgment to themselves*?

A. It means so to eat as to expose themselves to the displeasure of God, and thus to suffering.

THEREFORE,

Q. 97. What is required to the worthy receiving of the Lord's Supper?

It is required of them that would worthily partake of the Lord's Supper, that they examine themselves of their knowledge to discern the Lord's body, of their faith to feed upon him; of their repentance, love, and new obedience; lest, coming unworthily, they eat and drink judgment to themselves.

OF THE NATURE OF PRAYER

Q. What sort of an offering is prayer?

A. *Prayer is an offering up of our desires unto God.* It is telling him what we desire.

Q. What may we desire, and ask for, in prayer to God?

A. *For things agreeable to his will*; for such things as he is willing to grant to us.

Q. May we come in our own name or in Christ's name?
A. *In the name of Christ*; asking things on his account, for his sake, for the sake of what he has done for us as a Savior.

Q. What are our desires, in prayer, to be connected with?
A. *With confession of our sins, and thankful acknowledgement of his mercies.*

THEREFORE,

Q. 98. What is prayer?

Prayer is an offering up of our desires unto God, for things agreeable to his will, in the name of Christ, with confession of our sins, and thankful, acknowledgment of his mercies.

RULE FOR PRAYER

Q. What is of use to *direct us in prayer*?
A. *The whole Word of God.*

Q. What is the *special rule of direction*?

A. It is *that form of prayer which Christ taught his disciples.*

Q. What is that form *commonly called*?
A. *The Lord's Prayer*; because he composed it for his disciples.

THEREFORE,

Q. 99. What rule has God given for our direction in prayer?

The whole Word of God is of use to direct us in prayer; but the special rule of direction is that form of prayer which Christ taught his disciples, commonly called, "The Lord's Prayer."

OF THE PREFACE TO THE LORD'S PRAYER

Q. Which is the *preface* of the Lord's Prayer?
A. It is, *Our Father which art in heaven.*

Q. What does this preface teach us?
A. It *teaches us to draw near to God with all holy reverence and confidence*; with proper fear, and yet with hope of having a kind answer to our prayer.

Q. How, further, are we to draw near to God?

A. *As children to a Father, able and ready to help us.*

Q. What else does the *preface* teach us?
A. It teaches us *that we should pray with and for others;* that we should not only pray by ourselves and for ourselves, hut for others, and in company with others.

THEREFORE,

Q. 100. What does the preface of the Lord's Prayer teach us?

The preface of the Lord's prayer (which is, "Our Father which art in heaven"), teaches us to draw near to God with all holy reverence and confidence, as children to a father, able and ready to help us; and that we should pray with and for others.

OF THE FIRST PETITION

Q. Which is the first petition, or thing asked for?
A. It is, *Hallowed be thy name.*

Q. *In the first petition* what do we pray?
A. *We pray that God would enable us and others to glorify him.*

Q. In what respects should we glorify, or honor him?
A. *In all that whereby he makes himself known.*

Q. What else, in this first petition, do we ask for?
A. *That he would dispose all things to his own glory*; that he would make all things honor him.

T H E R E F O R E,

Q. 101. What do we pray for in the first petition?

In the first petition (which is, "Hallowed be thy name"), we pray that God would enable us and others to glorify him in all that whereby he makes himself known; and that he would dispose all things to his own glory.

OF THE SECOND PETITION

Q. Which is the second petition?
A. It is, *Thy kingdom come.*

Q. *In the second petition* what do we pray?
A. *We pray that Satan's kingdom may be destroyed*; that is, that Satan's power and bad influence over us and others may be brought to an end.

Q. Concerning what other *kingdom* do we pray?

A. We pray that the *kingdom of grace may be advanced*; that is, that Christ may have more persons to serve him, and that all who now serve him may do it more faithfully.

Q. When, therefore, is the *kingdom of grace* advanced?

A. When *ourselves and others* are *brought into it and kept in it*; when we become and continue the willing subjects and servants of Christ.

Q. What else does this second petition include?

A. *That the kingdom of glory may be hastened*; that the time may come when we and others shall be admitted into heaven; that bright and happy place, where God is honored by all in the highest and best manner.

THEREFORE,

Q. 102. What do we pray for in the second petition?

In the second petition (which is, "Thy kingdom come"), we pray that Satan's kingdom may be destroyed; and that the kingdom of grace may be advanced, ourselves and others brought into it, and kept in it; and that the kingdom of glory may be hastened.

Q. Which is the third petition?
A. It is. *Thy will be done in earth, as it is in heaven.*

Q. *In the third petition* what do we pray for?
A. *We pray that God, by his grace, would make its able and willing to know, obey, and submit to his will.*

Q. How far?
A. *In all things, as the angels do in heaven.*

THEREFORE,

Q. 103. What do we pray for in the third petition?

In the third petition (which is, "Thy will be done in earth, as it is in heaven"), we pray that God, by his grace, would make us able and willing to know, obey, and submit to his will in all things, as the angels do in heaven.

Q. Which is the fourth petition?
A. It is, *Give us this day our daily bread.*

Q. *In the fourth petition* what do we pray for?

A. *We pray that we may receive a competent portion of the good things of this life*; that is, a sufficient and proper share of them.

Q. How receive them?

A. *Of God's free gift*; that is, as something which we do not in the least degree deserve.

Q. Do we, in this petition, ask of God only for the good things of this life?

A. We ask also that we may *enjoy his blessing with them*; that is, that he would make them useful to us.

THEREFORE,

Q. 104. What do we pray for in the fourth petition?

In the fourth petition (which is, "Give us this day our daily bread"), we pray that of God's free gift we may receive a competent portion of the good things of this life, and enjoy his blessing with them.

Q. Which is the fifth petition?

A. It is, *And forgive us our debts, as we forgive our debtors.*

Q. *In the fifth petition* what do we pray for?

A. *We pray that God would freely pardon all our sins;* that is, pardon them without any pay from us.

Q. For whose sake, then, do we ask him to pardon them?

A. *For Christ's sake;* for the sake of what he has done and suffered for us.

Q. By what are we *the rather encouraged to ask this?*

A. *Because, by his grace, we are enabled from the heart to forgive others;* that is, to treat them kindly, as if they had not wronged, or injured us.

THEREFORE,

Q. 105. What do we pray for in the fifth petition?

In the fifth petition (which is, "And forgive us our debts, as we forgive our debtors"), we pray that God, for Christ's sake, would freely pardon all our sins; which we are the rather encouraged to ask, because by his grace we are enabled from the heart to forgive others.

OF THE SIXTH PETITION

Q. Which is the sixth petition?

A. It is, *And lead us not into temptation, but deliver us from evil.*

Q. *In the sixth petition* what do we pray for?

A. *We pray that God would keep us from being tempted to sin*; that is, that God would keep us from being urged or persuaded to sin.

Q. What other thing do we therein ask for?

A. *That God would support and deliver us when we are tempted*; that he would preserve us from being led into actual sin when urged or inclined to commit it.

THEREFORE,

Q. 106. What do we pray for in the sixth petition?

In the sixth petition (which is, "And lead us not into temptation, but deliver us from evil"), we pray that God would either keep us from being tempted to sin: or support and deliver us when we are tempted.

OF THE CONCLUSION OF THE LORD'S PRAYER

Q. Which is the conclusion of the Lord's Prayer?

A. It is, *For thine is the kingdom, and the power, and the glory, forever, Amen.*

Q. What does the *conclusion*, or close, *of the Lord's Prayer* teach us?

A. *It teaches us to take our encouragement in prayer from God only;* to expect blessings from him only, in answer to prayer.

Q. What else does it teach us?

A. It teaches us, *in our prayers to praise him.*

Q. And how are we to praise him?

A. *Ascribing kingdom, power, and glory to him;* that is, declaring that these belong of right to him; that he is the highest king; that he has all power to give what we ask and what we need; that he has every perfection, and every excellence, and that these will be shown in answering the petitions of this prayer.

Q. Why do we say, *Amen*?

A. It is *in testimony of our desire and assurance to be heard*; it is an expression which means that we wish and expect to obtain what we have thus asked for.

THEREFORE,

Q. 107. What does the conclusion of the Lord's Prayer teach us?

The conclusion of the Lord's Prayer (which is, "For thine is the kingdom, and the power, and the glory, forever, Amen.") teaches us to take our encouragement in prayer from God only; and in our prayers to praise him, ascribing kingdom power, and glory to him. And in testimony of our desire and assurance to be heard, we say, Amen.

For additional titles from Ichthus Publications,
visit our website at:

www.ichthuspublications.com

Made in the USA
Middletown, DE
18 February 2023

25173972R00077